STAND FAST

God's Guidance
for Kingdom Living

Henry M. Morris III

INSTITUTE FOR
CREATION
RESEARCH

Dallas, Texas
ICR.org

Dr. Henry M. Morris III holds four earned degrees, including a D.Min. from Luther Rice Seminary and the Pres-
idents and Key Executives MBA from Pepperdine Univer-
sity. A former college professor, administrator, business
executive, and senior pastor, Dr. Morris is an articulate
and passionate speaker frequently invited to address
church congregations, college assemblies, and national
conferences. The eldest son of ICR's founder, Dr. Morris
has served for many years in conference and writing min-
istry. His love for the Word of God and passion for Christian maturity, coupled
with God's gift of teaching, have given Dr. Morris a broad and effective ministry
over the years. He has authored numerous articles and books, including *The Big
Three: Major Events that Changed History Forever; Exploring the Evidence for Creation; 5
Reasons to Believe in Recent Creation; The Book of Beginnings; Pulling Down Strongholds:
Achieving Spiritual Victory through Strategic Offense; A Firm Foundation: Devotional Insights to Help You Know, Believe, and Defend Truth; Six Days of Creation; Your Origins
Matter; Unlocking the Mysteries of Genesis;* and *Places to Walk.* He is also a contrib-
utor to *Guide to Creation Basics, Creation Basics & Beyond,* and *Guide to the Universe.*

STAND FAST
God's Guidance for Kingdom Living

by Henry M. Morris III, D. Min.

First printing: November 2018

All Scripture quotations are from the New King James Version.

ISBN: 978-1-946246-26-4

Please visit our website for other books and resources: ICR.org

Printed in the United States of America.

TABLE OF CONTENTS

INTRODUCTION

One of the Bible's most frequently repeated messages is that the people of God's Kingdom must expect to "swim upstream" against the majority of humanity. Jesus said it best when He spoke about the difficulty of entering into Kingdom life:

> "Enter by the narrow gate; for wide is the gate and broad is the way that leads to destruction, and there are many who go in by it. Because narrow is the gate and difficult is the way which leads to life, and there are few who find it." (Matthew 7:13-14)

After God destroyed the first age with the horrible global Flood of Noah's day, everything the Lord did was so that "He might redeem us from every lawless deed and purify for Himself His own special people, zealous for good works" (Titus 2:14). But those special people would always be opposed by the great Adversary who "walks about like a roaring lion, seeking whom he may devour" (1 Peter 5:8).

God's people will constantly deal with those who are under the power of the Devil. Such a one "does not stand in the truth, because there is no truth in him. When he speaks a lie, he speaks from his own resources, for he is a liar and the father of it" (John 8:44). Thankfully, the twice-born "are of God...and have overcome them, because He who is in you is greater than he who is in the world" (1 John 4:4).

This little book reviews some of the precious passages of Scripture that provide a source of encouragement for God's redeemed people, as well as the responsibilities, warnings, and promises that shelter our life in Christ.

✑ 1 ✑

INSTRUCTIONS AND RESPONSIBILITIES

The Bible provides a number of commands and clear statements of our responsibilities as the special people of God. This little book can't possibly list them all, but here's a quick overview of what we must do.

- *"Stand fast* in the faith, be brave, be strong"* (1 Corinthians 16:13).

- *"Stand fast* therefore in the liberty by which Christ has made us free, and do not be entangled again with a yoke of bondage"* (Galatians 5:1).

- *"Stand fast* in one spirit, with one mind striving together for the faith of the gospel"* (Philippians 1:27).

- *"Stand fast* and hold the traditions which you were taught, whether by word or our epistle"* (2 Thessalonians 2:15).

There is much more involved in the Christian life, but our Lord Jesus has given us "all things that pertain to life and godliness, through the knowledge of Him who called us" (2 Peter 1:3). Keep this in mind and be encouraged as we take a look at the instructions given in God's Word that make our responsibilities clear.

STAND FAST

"Therefore, my beloved and longed-for brethren, my joy and crown, so stand fast in the Lord, beloved." (Philippians 4:1)

Several adjectives precede the command contained in this text. Not only does Paul twice use "beloved" to describe his relationship with the Philippians, but he also insists that he "longs for" them and anticipates joy at the recognition of the crown he will receive in heaven.

These are intense words. *Agapetos* is the descriptive Greek term translated as "beloved." The heavenly Father uses *agapetos* to express His love for His "beloved Son" (Matthew 3:17). Most authors of the New Testament letters freely use *agapetos* to describe various personal relationships with their brothers and sisters in Christ. That unique and deeply spiritual love is what demonstrates our difference to the unsaved (John 13:34-35).

Since Paul is separated from the Philippian church (probably writing the letter from Rome), his love for them caused him to "long for [them] all with the affection of Jesus Christ" (Philippians 1:8). That passionate ache is mitigated by the joy coming from the certain knowledge that his work among them will result in a victor's crown (Greek *stephanos*) when God rewards our service. "For what is our hope, or joy, or crown of rejoicing? Is it not even you in the presence of our Lord Jesus Christ at His coming?" (1 Thessalonians 2:19).

So, "stand fast in one spirit, with one mind striving together for the faith of the gospel" (Philippians 1:27). "Watch, stand fast in the faith, be strong" (1 Corinthians 16:13). Stand fast in the "liberty by which Christ has made us free, and do not be entangled again with a yoke of bondage" (Galatians 5:1). "For now we live, if you stand fast in the Lord" (1 Thessalonians 3:8).

CONTEND EARNESTLY

"I found it necessary to write to you exhorting you to contend earnestly for the faith which was once for all delivered to the saints." (Jude 1:3)

A
fter Jude had responded to the Holy Spirit's prompting to direct his thoughts away from writing a gospel account, the intensity of the growing battle for "the faith" came into focus. Perhaps Jude was aware of Paul's observation that we do not "wrestle" against ordinary forces, but our battle deals with the "spiritual hosts of wickedness in the heavenly places" (Ephesians 6:12).

The special word that was chosen by the Holy Spirit to speak to this struggle in Jude's letter was *epagonizomai*. The core word (*agonizomai*) is used in the famous passage "I have fought the good fight, I have finished the race, I have kept the faith" (2 Timothy 4:7). Paul also notes what "great conflict" he felt for the church at Colosse (Colossians 2:1) and that Epaphras was "always laboring fervently" for them in his prayers (Colossians 4:12).

The object of this spiritual struggle was "the faith which was once for all delivered to the saints." Two matters are of importance in that little phrase. First, "the faith" is a specific designation used in the New Testament to incorporate the basic doctrines of the New Covenant. It includes, but does not limit itself to, the belief that results in salvation. The early churches were "strengthened in the faith" (Acts 16:5). We are to "stand fast in the faith" (1 Corinthians 16:13) and to come to a "unity of the faith" (Ephesians 4:13).

Second, that body of doctrine was "once for all delivered to the saints." Implicit in that comment is the responsibility of the Holy Spirit to "guide [the apostles] into all truth" (John 16:13). Both Old and New Testaments insist that we are not to add or subtract from the words of God's Word. Jude's epistle emphasizes the awful judgment that comes upon those who would distort or disdain what is "the faith."

HOLD FAST

"Hold fast the pattern of sound words which you have heard from me, in faith and love which are in Christ Jesus." (2 Timothy 1:13)

There are several significant pieces to this important command. We must "hold fast" to the pattern of the "sound words" that have been given to us—and that firm hold must rest in the faith and love we have in Christ Jesus.

This is not an option. We are to hold to the form of the sound words. *Hupotuposis* is the Greek term. We are to be "under" (*hupo*) the outline or "pattern" (*tupos*) of the wholesome words. *Hupotuposis* is only used one other time in the New Testament, where Paul insists that his life was to be "a *pattern* to those who are going to believe on Him" (1 Timothy 1:16). The purpose of the two letters to Timothy is to encourage the young pastor to follow the example of his human teacher Paul, who completely submitted himself to the authority of all Scripture.

To the Roman Christians, Paul was delighted that they "obeyed from the heart that *form* of doctrine to which [they] were delivered" (Romans 6:17). To the Corinthians, he reminded them that the events recorded in the life of Israel had "happened to them as *examples*" (1 Corinthians 10:11). Paul also insisted to the church at Philippi that they should "follow my example, and note those who so walk, as you have us for a *pattern*" (Philippians 3:17).

Both biblical and church history provide us with patterns to follow. But the sound words of Scripture give what is "profitable for doctrine, for reproof, for correction, for instruction in righteousness, that the man of God may be complete, thoroughly equipped for every good work" (2 Timothy 3:16-17).

BUILD YOURSELF UP

"But you, beloved, building yourselves up on your most holy faith, praying in the Holy Spirit, keep yourselves in the love of God, looking for the mercy of our Lord Jesus Christ unto eternal life." (Jude 1:20-21)

The New Testament relationship of the twice-born to the eternal condition is compared to a building of God (Ephesians 2:22) made up of "living stones" (1 Peter 2:5). Thus, there is often the exhortation for us to build a holy association with each other (Romans 14:19) and to seek to build a strong assembly as we work together (Ephesians 4:16).

Each of the many references uses some combination of descriptive preposition or adjective along with the term for house. The general application assumes that since we will be "housed" together in eternity, we should seek to be building that house while on Earth. Even those who are in authority in the "house of God" (1 Timothy 3:15) are to be focused on building that house (Ephesians 4:11-12).

Jude addresses the individual. He presumes we are aware that we are "built on the foundation of the apostles and prophets" with "Jesus Christ Himself being the chief cornerstone" (Ephesians 2:20). Even with a "wise master builder" like Paul to give us inspired instructions (1 Corinthians 3:10), we need to be very careful how we build on the foundation that Jesus Christ has laid for us. Our work can be "gold, silver, precious stones, wood, hay, [or] straw," and will be evaluated by the "fire" of God's timeless judgment (1 Corinthians 3:12-13).

The construction of the building—both the larger house and the individual "living stones" that make up the house—are to be built up on the "most holy faith." Once the foundation has been laid by Jesus Christ, we are to be "rooted and built up in Him and established in the faith, as you have been taught, abounding in it with thanksgiving" (Colossians 2:7).

BE STRONG IN GRACE

*"You therefore, my son, be strong in the grace
that is in Christ Jesus." (2 Timothy 2:1)*

In the Old Testament, "grace" (used 69 times) is often applied in the sense of personal favors or physical blessings. "For the LORD God is a sun and shield; the LORD will give grace and glory; no good thing will He withhold from those who walk uprightly" (Psalm 84:11). In the New Testament, however, the term (used 156 times) often seems to emphasize God's personal empowerment or the granting of His unique spiritual favor, as is clear in the wonderful passage Ephesians 2:8-9: "For by grace you have been saved through faith, and that not of yourselves; it is the gift of God, not of works, lest anyone should boast."

Once the saving grace has been given, the believer is expected to use that grace with victory in mind—a confidence that empowers our spiritual life and witness. We are to be "strong in the grace that is in Christ Jesus."

Hence, we are to "be strong in the Lord and in the power of His might" (Ephesians 6:10) as we wrestle against the powers of darkness that battle us unceasingly. Although "[we] can do all things through Christ who strengthens [us]" (Philippians 4:13), we must remember that those "things" include the entire spectrum from poverty to wealth, and from hunger to satisfaction. God's grace is strong enough to counter every worldly circumstance.

We must remember, however, that even the greatest heroes of the faith endured intense opposition, seasons of pain and privation, and occasionally were tortured to death (Hebrews 11:32-38). God's strong grace is sufficient. "Therefore I take pleasure in infirmities, in reproaches, in needs, in persecutions, in distresses, for Christ's sake. For when I am weak, then I am strong" (2 Corinthians 12:10).

WORK OUT YOUR SALVATION

*"Therefore, my beloved, as you have always obeyed, not as in my
presence only, but now much more in my absence, work out
your own salvation with fear and trembling." (Philippians 2:12)*

This verse is sometimes used by those who would insist that our salvation requires "works" either to obtain or to maintain the "new birth." Even a casual reading of the New Testament does not support that view (John 5:24; 6:37; 2 Corinthians 5:21; Ephesians 4:24; etc.).

This passage, both in context and by specific word choices of the Holy Spirit, is focused on what we are to do with our salvation—obey and produce! The writer of the Hebrews letter spoke of "things that accompany salvation" (Hebrews 6:9). And even the Old Testament prophet Isaiah insisted that we should "draw water from the wells of salvation" (Isaiah 12:3).

Two parables speak specifically to this work: the gift of the talents and the gift of the minas. God illustrated His grace by the gift of "talents" (Matthew 25:14-30) to His workers, as well as His expectation of their productivity for the profit of the Owner. Differing amounts were given to the servants based on their abilities, and judgment was based on their efficiency, or the percentage of their return.

In the gift of the minas (Luke 19:13-27), God is the investor and His servants are all of us who receive (John 1:12) the gift of salvation. What we do with this gift is our responsibility. The same amount was given to each servant, without the mention of abilities. Judgment was then based on the servant's effectiveness, or gain.

It is no wonder, then, that Paul exhorts us to "work out" the priceless salvation that has been given to us with "fear and trembling." God is working in us, and He expects us to "will and to do His good pleasure" (Philippians 2:13).

BE LIGHTS IN THE WORLD

*"...children of God without fault in the midst
of a crooked and perverse generation, among whom
you shine as lights in the world." (Philippians 2:15)*

The Hebrew and Greek terms for "sons [i.e., children] of God" are essentially the same, but the Old Testament always uses the phrase in reference to angels, whereas the New Testament always references the twice-born saints of God.

This text emphasizes the precise reason our Lord Jesus prayed "I do not pray that You should take them out of the world....They are not of the world, just as I am not of the world" (John 17:15-16). We who share this marvelous relationship bear both the "love the Father has bestowed on us" and the unique rejection that "the world does not know us, because it did not know Him" (1 John 3:1).

Jesus said, "I am the light of the world" (John 8:12), and we who are His disciples are "the light of the world" (Matthew 5:14). We, unlike the angels, are to remain in this unfair and distorted world as lights. Consider this! We are the light that the Lord Jesus left in this world to represent Him and His message after He returned to heaven (John 9:5).

That is why the Scriptures refer to us as saints (holy ones) and disciples (followers); even the pejorative "Christians" (Acts 11:26) identifies us as representing the King! We must therefore shine with the truth (John 3:19) and shed the "light of the gospel of the glory of Christ" (2 Corinthians 4:4), attempting to give "light to every man coming into the world" (John 1:9).

Finally, we are surely commanded to "walk in the light as He is in the light" (1 John 1:7). Our light should never be covered under a "basket" (Matthew 5:15) but be set on a "hill" for all to see (Matthew 5:14).

2

ALERTS AND COUNSELS

The opening song of the book of Psalms begins:

Blessed is the man who walks not in the counsel of the ungodly, nor stands in the path of sinners, nor sits in the seat of the scornful; but his delight is in the law of the LORD, and in His law he meditates day and night. (Psalm 1:1-2)

The promise of happiness is for those of the Lord's people who do not listen to or become enamored with the counsel of those of the Adversary but who instead have a longing pleasure in the Word of God. It would be less than helpful if God had charged us with the responsibly to stand fast and contend earnestly for His Kingdom and not given us insight on how to spot those who are "enemies of the cross of Christ" (Philippians 3:18).

The prophet Jeremiah quoted from Psalm 1 and added a wonderful application to the happiness that was promised.

"Blessed is the man who trusts in the LORD, and whose hope is the LORD. For he shall be like a tree planted by the waters, which spreads out its roots by the river, and will not fear when heat comes; but its leaf will be green, and will not be anxious in the year of drought, nor will cease from yielding fruit." (Jeremiah 17:7-8)

That is worth whatever resistance we might face when we stand fast as we put the Kingdom first in our lives. The final fulfillment of those promises may ultimately be achieved only in the "new heavens and a new earth" (2 Peter 3:13). But even if that is the only time we see God's blessing, we are told to "rejoice and be exceedingly glad, for great is your reward in heaven, for so they persecuted the prophets who were before you" (Matthew 5:12).

Following is a sample of the alerts and counsels the Lord has provided for us.

DO NOT LOVE THE WORLD'S THINGS

"Do not love the world or the things in the world." (1 John 2:15)

W e must be wary of the world's things, because we are "in the world," not "of the world" (John 17:11-16). The command in our text is that we are not to love the world or its things, not that we should remain blissfully ignorant of them. We are to be "wise as serpents and harmless as doves" (Matthew 10:16).

There are big things of the world like nations and kingdoms (Matthew 4:8; Luke 12:30) as well as cares and riches (Mark 4:19) that can sap our focus and drain our loyalties. And there are "principles" and "elements" (Colossians 2:20; Galatians 4:3) that can twist our thinking and "cheat" us (Colossians 2:8).

We are warned that friendship with the worldly lifestyle and that which espouses the things of the world make us an enemy of God (James 4:4). That is because such people embrace the "spirit of the world" and not "the Spirit who is from God" (1 Corinthians 2:12). Those people speak about the things of the world, and the world listens to them (1 John 4:5).

God's people may be base, weak, and even foolish in the eyes of the world (1 Corinthians 1:27-28). Since the great Creator God has chosen us out of the world (John 15:19), it should not surprise us that the world hates those who belong to the Lord Jesus (John 17:14). Hence, the ungodly passion that drives the ungodly behavior of the world—"the lust of the flesh, and the lust of the eyes, and the pride of life—is not of the Father, but is of the world" (1 John 2:16).

Those passions and the people who embrace them will pass away. But "he who does the will of God abides forever" (1 John 2:17).

IDENTIFY THE ANTICHRISTS

"Little children, it is the last hour; and as you have heard
that the Antichrist is coming, even now many antichrists have come,
by which we know that it is the last hour." (1 John 2:18)

Evangelicals expect "the" Antichrist to be revealed in the future, yet there are more warnings about "many" antichrists who are currently and actively plotting evil. John lists two specific identifying factors that enable us to spot these "anti" Christs.

"Who is a liar but he who denies that Jesus is the Christ? He is antichrist who denies the Father and the Son" (1 John 2:22).

"And every spirit that does not confesses that Jesus Christ has come in the flesh is not of God. And this is the spirit of the Antichrist…[who] is now already in the world" (1 John 4:3).

This much is clear. Anyone who refuses to accept the incarnated Christ as the Son of God is *anti*-Christ. Perhaps we need to see this term in its simplicity. Those who are "anti" Christ (oppose, reject, over against, opposite to, before, instead of, in place of) are antichrists!

Peter warns that false prophets and false teachers are also "anti" Christ—and that they may well come from among the Lord's visible Kingdom.

"But there were also false prophets among the people, even as there will be false teachers among you, who will secretly bring in destructive heresies, even denying the Lord who bought them, and bring on themselves swift destruction" (2 Peter 2:1).

Thus, we are told that Satan's "ministers also transform themselves into ministers of righteousness" (2 Corinthians 11:15). No wonder we should have caution! These are the last days, and we need to be alert!

GUARD THE WORD

*"You are my portion, O LORD; I have said
that I would keep Your words." (Psalm 119:57)*

Three stanzas within the 22 stanzas of Psalm 119 have all eight Hebrew terms used to describe the Word of God. How appropriate it is that the central theme in these verses (vv. 57-64) provides us succinct ways to keep (guard) His Word.

Principally, our whole heart must be involved in seeking the "favor" of God (v. 58). The greatest commandment (Matthew 22:38) rests on loving God with all of our hearts. If we seek God's blessing, both during our earthly life and in the eternity to come, we will "trust in the LORD with all your heart, and lean not on your own understanding; in all your ways acknowledge Him, and He shall direct your paths" (Proverbs 3:5-6).

Such a heart thinks (considers, reckons) about the ways of God and turns (turns back, corrects) its "feet to [His] testimonies" (Psalm 119:59). The godly life is not an unplanned life. The godly life seeks to understand and obey the words of God. Such a life makes "haste" and will not delay keeping His commandments (v. 60).

Circumstances may cause temporary difficulties in the lives of godly people (v. 61), but they will not forget the laws of God. Rather, they will rise at "midnight" (the deepest time of trouble) to give thanks to the Lord "because of [His] righteous judgments" (v. 62).

The one who wants to guard the Word of God is a companion of those who fear God and who keep the precepts of the Word (v. 63). The godly heart sees the mercy of the Lord everywhere and longs for the "Creator of the ends of the earth" (Isaiah 40:28) to teach him the eternal statutes of His Word (Psalm 119:64). May "such a heart" (Deuteronomy 5:29) be ours as we seek to serve Him.

Long for the Word

*"My soul faints for Your salvation, but I hope in Your
word. My eyes fail from searching Your word, saying,
'When will You comfort me?'" (Psalm 119:81-82)*

Those who love the Lord with all their heart, soul, and might (Deuteronomy 6:5) and those who seek the Kingdom of God (Matthew 6:33) deeply long to "understand the fear of the Lord, and find the knowledge of God" (Proverbs 2:5).

Yet in spite of such longing, the saints of God are often perplexed by the apparent success of the wicked. The writer of Psalm 119 was no exception:

- "When will You comfort me?" (v. 82).
- "I have become like a wineskin in smoke" (v. 83).
- "When will You execute judgment on those who persecute me?" (v. 84).
- "The proud have dug pits for me" (v. 85).
- "They persecute me wrongfully" (v. 86).
- "They almost made an end of me on earth" (v. 87).

Among all the heartfelt complaints, however, is a continual reliance on the promises and principles of God's Word. The psalmist promised not to forget God's statutes even though he felt invisible to God (v. 83). And though he knew his days were not guaranteed, he still expected God to bring judgment on the wicked (v. 84). He knew the "commandments are faithful" and promises the Lord he will not forsake the "precepts" (vv. 86-87).

The final request should be ours as well: "Revive me according to Your lovingkindness" (v. 88). Even though God has "shown me great and severe troubles," the confidence is that God "shall revive me again" (Psalm 71:20). On the basis of that assurance, our response should be like this godly man's: "So that I may keep the testimony of Your mouth" (Psalm 119:88).

BE IN SYNC WITH GOD'S PEOPLE

"Fulfill my joy by being like-minded, having the same love,
being of one accord, of one mind." (Philippians 2:2)

This emphatic command, along with the parallel terms, helps us understand the concept of "thinking" the same thing. "Be of the same mind toward one another. Do not set your mind on high things, but associate with the humble. Do not be wise in your own opinion" (Romans 12:16).

Such thinking also includes "having the same love." There are two aspects of this love. First, the term itself (*agape*) would demand that all of Christ's disciples "love one another, for love is of God" (1 John 4:7). This is often repeated to the twice-born so that our love for each other is so obvious that "by this all will know that you are My disciples" (John 13:35).

Godly love then produces "being of one accord." This phrase is the translation of the Greek word *sumpsuchos*, which is a compound of the preposition most often translated "with" and the word for "soul." Thus, the *agape* that we are to share results in a connection "with-soul" that binds the like-mindedness in agreement with the mind and spirit of the Creator God.

We are finally commanded to be of "one mind," slightly different from the "like-minded" opening charge of Philippians 2:2. The initial words are *auto phroneô*—"his thinking." The last use is *en phroneô*—one (way of) thinking.

The entire context of the opening verses of Philippians 2 is to think like Jesus Christ thinks. "Let this mind be in you, which was also in Christ Jesus" (Philippians 2:5). "Set your affection [*phroneô*] on things above, not on things on the earth" (Colossians 3:2). This kind of thinking must have God's love and soul embedded in the very core of our heart, soul, mind, and strength.

PAY ATTENTION TO GOD'S LEADERS

"The things which you learned and received and heard and saw in me, these do, and the God of peace will be with you." (Philippians 4:9)

From earliest childhood, we learn by watching the actions and lives of others. First, of course, our parents, then our peers and educators, politicians, business leaders, musicians, celebrities—the list is nearly endless. We learn by what we receive, hear, and see.

Jesus said, "They shall all be taught by God" (John 6:45). The foundational learning process that enables the receiving and hearing of further truth must come first from God, through His Word and by His twice-born. Paul's young protégé, Timothy, first learned from his mother and grandmother about God, and then under Paul's tutelage from the Scriptures (2 Timothy 1:5; 3:15).

But the key to learning is active attention! One must first receive, hear, and see. Paul commended the Thessalonians because they "received the word of God which you heard from us, you welcomed it not as the word of men, but as it is in truth, the word of God" (1 Thessalonians 2:13). The Bereans were "more fair-minded" because they "searched the Scriptures daily" (Acts 17:11). The wise preacher "pondered and sought out and set in order many proverbs" (Ecclesiastes 12:9).

Information, however well absorbed, is worthless without applying what is learned. The philosophers of Athens were scorned because they "spent their time in nothing else but either to tell or to hear some new thing" (Acts 17:21). All of us must first be learners. Soon, however, we must work out our "own salvation with fear and trembling," since God has chosen to work through us (Philippians 2:12-13).

BE GENEROUS WITH YOUR RESOURCES

*"Nevertheless you have done well that you
shared in my distress." (Philippians 4:14)*

The King James Version uses the word "communicate" for the term translated here as "share." Our use of "communicate" today normally means speaking, understanding one another, or simply passing on instructions. The Greek word is *sugkoinoneo*, a compound of the preposition "with" and the primary word for "participation."

The basic term is often translated "partner" or "partake" and is frequently connected with the act of sharing finances in the ministry of others. That is the application in the context of this verse. Paul commends the Philippian church for "partnering" with him in his journeys and recognizing time and again what was needed for the success of the ministry.

Today, there are a vast array of charity-based organizations, from large hospitals and universities to local food and clothing distribution efforts. Most of these, by the way, were started by Christian groups as a way to "communicate" to the distress of many. But how do we determine who among the many, or at what ratio, to attempt to distribute "to the needs of the saint" (Romans 12:13)?

Two main principles must guide our "communication" in the Kingdom. First, it is clear that our New Testament responsibility is first to the church in which our Lord has placed us. Some disagree, but storehouse tithing appears to claim our first priority. Then there is the opportunity to follow the specific leading of God among those ministries with which we are familiar and who we are confident "seek first the kingdom of God" (Matthew 6:33).

KNOW YOUR CO-WORKERS

"And I urge you also, true companion, help these women who labored with me in the gospel, with Clement also, and the rest of my fellow workers, whose names are in the Book of Life." (Philippians 4:3)

The King James Version renders "companion" as "yokefellow," which provides an interesting insight into the relationship between fellow believers. Although "yokefellow" is out of use today, the meaning is easily understood. Most of us know a yoke is designed to connect two animals together to increase the power to accomplish the work that needs to be done.

Jesus said, "Take My yoke upon you and learn from Me, for I am gentle and lowly in heart, and you will find rest for your souls. For My yoke is easy and My burden is light" (Matthew 11:29-30). From a spiritual perspective, we labor together with the Lord Jesus. Among ourselves, we labor in the gospel. It is worth noting that God sees the marriage bond as "joined together" (same term) with a yoke (Matthew 19:6).

Interestingly, as Paul speaks highly of the women who labored with him, he uses two very different concepts to recognize their contribution. First, he describes them as *sunathleo*, those who are "engaged in the contest" with him, like someone who "competes in athletics" (2 Timothy 2:5). Then, Paul uses *sunergos* to describe those who have accomplished meaningful work alongside him. Titus is described as Paul's "partner and fellow worker" (2 Corinthians 8:23). These women had evidently earned Paul's respect for their commitment to the Kingdom work.

Although the picture drawn by these synonyms rests on the work aspect, surely there is the assumption that those who are yoked together are anticipating a common goal. Jesus, with "the joy that was set before Him," endured the "work" of the cross (Hebrews 12:2). We labor in the Kingdom since our names are "in the Book of Life."

RIGHTLY DIVIDE THE WORD

"Be diligent to present yourself approved to God, a worker who does not need to be ashamed, rightly dividing the word of truth." (2 Timothy 2:15)

This command is for us to "be diligent" (Greek *spoudazo*) for God's approval by "rightly dividing" the word of truth. That which is to be rightly divided is not in doubt: "Sanctify them by Your truth. Your word is truth" (John 17:17). The end goal is to "present yourself" as one who is, therefore, approved by God.

The key is to rightly divide the Scriptures. The Greek word *orthotomeo*, only used this one time, has several shades of meaning: to cut straight, to cut straight ways, to proceed on straight paths, to hold a straight course, to make straight and smooth, to handle aright, to teach the truth directly and correctly.

Two passages emphasize the way to "divide" the Scriptures. When Isaiah asked rhetorical questions about how to learn and understand biblical knowledge, the answer was "precept must be upon precept, precept upon precept, line upon line, line upon line, here a little, there a little" (Isaiah 28:9-10). Thus:

Find the major pieces first.

Find the supporting elements next.

Find the pieces throughout the text.

The "wise preacher" Solomon noted that one who would teach people knowledge must have "pondered and sought out and set in order many proverbs" (Ecclesiastes 12:9).

Pay attention to the words (meanings, context).

Penetrate (research) the teaching (text first, then books).

Organize the information for teaching purposes.

This kind of study preparation requires a "worker"—one who is willing to give the diligence necessary to produce teachings built on the "word of truth." If properly prepared, such a worker will never be ashamed.

BEWARE!

"Beware lest anyone cheat you through philosophy and empty deceit, according to the tradition of men, according to the basic principles of the world, and not according to Christ." (Colossians 2:8)

I n spite of the resources available to the twice-born—and in spite of assurance, order, steadfastness, a good walk that is rooted and built up in Him—it is still possible for a Christian to be plundered by the world's crafty message. We can "fall from [our] own steadfastness" (2 Peter 3:17) or even lose "those things we worked for" (2 John 1:8).

The one who "cheats" a believer will use *philosophia*, a Greek word that means "fond of wisdom." It is used only one other time in the New Testament, in Acts 17:18 of the philosophers on Mars Hill. Interestingly, the biblical word for "wisdom" is most often used in a negative way when referring to man's wisdom. "Has not God made foolish the wisdom of this world" (1 Corinthians 1:20)? Believers can be robbed of their steadfastness in Christ if they become fond of the wisdom of the world.

The cheater also uses "empty deceit" and the "tradition of men" to plunder the believer. Jesus castigated the Pharisees because they had "made the commandment of God of no effect by [their] tradition.... teaching as doctrines the commandments of men" (Matthew 15:6, 9). Paul warned Timothy that he must avoid "profane and idle babblings and contradictions of what is falsely called knowledge—by professing it some have strayed concerning the faith" (1 Timothy 6:20-21).

The robber will even use the "principles of the world." The term used for principles means "to belong to a series, to be in rank, or to come to an agreement." Essentially, this technique is using logic to prove a point, securing a change of mind. We are told the world's principles will cheat us when the logic is "not according to Christ."

HIDDEN ROCKS

*"These are spots in your love feasts, while they feast with you
without fear, serving only themselves." (Jude 1:12)*

T he "spots" that the translators chose for this description by
Jude may be better understood as "hidden rocks" just below
a lake's surface or covered over by shallow sand in a pathway.
Spilas is the Greek word, not used elsewhere in the New Testament.

The love feasts Jude refers to are somewhat difficult to describe
biblically since this is the only time the word *agape* is used in the
plural. There is some evidence that the early churches were extending
the time of celebration of the Lord's Supper improperly (1 Corinthians 11:20-21), and it is probable that his warning would apply to
churches who are indifferent to maintaining purity (1 Corinthians
11:27-29).

But the imagery also appears to express the danger the "spots"
present amidst the loving environment of most churches. Jude gives
several insights about the character of those who would resist the faith.
These people have established themselves as they feast and are feasting
"without fear." The word choices are powerful.

The spots are *suneuocheo* (feeding with) and getting along very well
with the rest of the church, shepherding themselves (*poimaino*) boldly
(*aphobos*). This is bad! These evil men have become so entrenched that
they lead their own faction with no fear of resistance or confrontation.
The Lord Jesus has stern words to speak to those churches who allow
biblical error to establish itself through false teachers and unconcerned
leaders (Revelation 2 and 3).

Peter describes such people as "spots and blemishes, carousing in
their own deceptions while they feast with you...that cannot cease
from sin, enticing unstable souls" (2 Peter 2:13-14). Not a pretty
picture. God does not tolerate such ungodly behavior, and neither
should we.

WATERLESS CLOUDS

"Woe unto them!... They are clouds without water,
carried about by the winds." (Jude 1:12)

This appears to be the only reference in the Bible that compares clouds to people. Several references use cloud imagery to depict the presence of God directing Israel (Exodus 13:21), speaking to Moses (Exodus 16:10-11), anointing the tabernacle (Exodus 40:34-38) and the temple (1 Kings 8:10-11), and speaking to the apostles on the Mount of Transfiguration (Matthew 17:5). Our Lord Jesus was taken up to heaven in a cloud (Acts 1:9) and will return in a cloud as well (Luke 21:27).

Here, however, Jude applies a strong negative imagery. Those who introduce evil into the Lord's churches may seem to represent the presence of God, but their misty vapor holds no "water"—and it will only obscure the brilliance of light and obfuscate the real "temperature" of the environment.

In an agrarian-based economy, clouds were hopeful signs of rain to refresh the land. Some of that positive view has been lost by urban societies, which often see rain as an inconvenience. New Testament imagery connects water with life-giving properties emanating from the Holy Spirit and with the cleansing value of the words of Scripture (John 4:14; Ephesians 5:26). Paul warned Titus about many "idle talkers and deceivers" who must be stopped so that the believers under his care would become "sound in the faith" (Titus 1:8-13).

Thus, Jude compares those who hinder "the faith" to those who appear to represent godly pursuits and character but are empty of the refreshing and guiding power of the Holy Spirit and void of biblical wisdom and insight. They are "tossed to and fro and carried about with every wind of doctrine" (Ephesians 4:14) and "do not serve our Lord Jesus Christ, but their own belly, and by smooth words and flattering speech deceive the hearts of the simple" (Romans 16:18).

FRUITLESS TREES

"Woe unto them!...[They are] late autumn trees without fruit,
twice dead, pulled up by the roots." (Jude 1:12)

M any illustrations in Scripture compare the responsibility of trees to bear fruit and the responsibility of Christians to produce righteousness. The reason for the frequent comparisons is that "a good tree does not bear bad fruit, nor does a bad tree bear good fruit" (Luke 6:43). It is easy to tell what kind a tree is because "every tree is known by its own fruit. For men do not gather figs from thorns, nor do they gather grapes from a bramble bush" (Luke 6:44).

Jude is making the point, however, that there are "trees" planted amidst the orchard of God's Kingdom churches that have withering fruit or have already been rooted up as worthless, fruitless, and twice-dead. These trees have absolutely no place among the healthy trees. At best they scar and mar the beauty of the orchard, and at worst they spread their decay and rot throughout it.

Another important point is that trees that have withered or cannot produce a good fruit are not salvageable. All of nature demonstrates and reinforces the eternal principle that "every good tree bears good fruit, but a bad tree bears bad fruit" (Matthew 7:17). Such dead, fruitless trees are to be "cut down and thrown into the fire" (Matthew 3:10).

The common thread in all of these several pictures by Jude is the damage that can be done by ungodly "tares" among the wheat (Matthew 13:24-30), fig trees that should be providing nourishment but do not (Luke 13:6-9), and plants that are choked by "the cares of this world [and] the deceitfulness of riches" (Mark 4:19). All of these can spread the "leaven" through the whole "lump" and undermine the work of God (Galatians 5:9).

RAGING WAVES

"They are…raging waves of the sea,
foaming up their own shame." (Jude 1:13)

J ude connects together a string of 21 illustrations to describe the character of ungodly people who are attacking "the faith which was once for all delivered to the saints" (v. 3). This very poignant letter literally sizzles with scathing imagery describing those who dare to stir up dissension and disobedience among God's people.

The particular image in verse 13 is of roiling billows surging ashore after a storm, spitting out "shame" from amidst the foam. The physical picture is disgusting enough. As the energy of the storm increases the waves' height and frequency, the detritus in and on the ocean is picked up and carried along. As the waves rise up toward the shore, they break, and the foam begins to collect and then spew out the "shame" previously covered by the depths.

Isaiah's comparison is most apt: "But the wicked are like the troubled sea, when it cannot rest, whose waters cast up mire and dirt" (Isaiah 57:20). The shame cast up by these raging waves is not just filthy but also damaging to those among whom the shame is dumped.

Paul warned the Corinthian church about those who dealt with "hidden things of shame," were "walking in craftiness," or were "handling the word of God deceitfully." In vivid contrast, Paul and his co-laborers openly displayed "the truth commending ourselves to every man's conscience in the sight of God" (2 Corinthians 4:2). Like Jude, Paul forecasts only destruction for these kinds of people. They brag "in their shame" and have their mind set on "earthly things" (Philippians 3:19).

Foaming at the mouth is frequently connected with demonic oppression in Scripture (Mark 9:17-18; Luke 9:39; etc.). Medically, the symptom is seldom positive. Perhaps Jude is offering a glimpse of the devilish source of such "raging" and raising a further alarm.

WANDERING STARS

This short reference is somewhat enigmatic. The five "wandering stars" of Mercury, Venus, Mars, Jupiter, and Saturn were clearly known in Jude's day, and their behavior had been plotted for many centuries. The Bible also uses "stars" as figures of speech for angelic beings in Job and Revelation.

It is clear in context that Jude is referencing ungodly people, most likely influential leaders in the churches who are damaging and defiling the work of the Kingdom. The particular focus of this example is that they are "reserved" for a "blackness of darkness forever."

Earlier, Jude cited "the angels who did not keep their proper domain" as being "reserved in everlasting chains under darkness for the judgment of the great day" (v. 6). Peter alludes to the same punishment of "angels who sinned" who were delivered "into chains of darkness, to be reserved for judgment" (2 Peter 2:4).

But it does not appear that Jude is speaking of angels in verse 13. Beginning in verse 8, Jude begins to tie his illustrations to people—leaders who are using their role and privileges for evil rather than good. All of the previous examples are obvious: filthy dreamers, natural beasts, those behaving like Cain, Balaam, or Korah. Even the waterless clouds, fruitless trees, and foaming waves are easily compared to human behavior.

How do we apply this illustration? Since the Creator made all things, His revealed Word often provides insight about the true nature of the universe long before we discover it. Comets were observed in Old Testament times. Today we know that they "wander" for some time but eventually dissipate into "the blackness of darkness forever." Just so, these "stars" may wow some for a season, but they are reserved for an eternity in hell.

GRUMBLERS AND COMPLAINERS

"These are grumblers, complainers, walking according
to their own lusts; and they mouth great swelling words,
flattering people to gain advantage." (Jude 1:16)

J ude's book cites several incidents in the early history of Israel that occurred right after they were wonderfully delivered from slavery in Egypt. Within a very short time, they had come through the Red Sea, had bitter water made sweet, seen water come out of a rock, and been fed with "angels' food" from heaven. Yet, when the 12 spies came back from the land of Canaan that had been promised to them, there was a widespread revolt against God and Moses' leadership.

The 10 spies who "grumbled" against God "died by the plague before the LORD" (Numbers 14:37). Some who had previously sided with the defeatist words of the spies tried to take matters into their own hands and "presumed to go up" to fight against the Canaanites and were killed or scattered (Numbers 14:44-45).

Much of the history of Israel is marked by various ways of turning away from God. Psalm 81 provides a good summary of how God sees this behavior: "I am the LORD your God, who brought you out of the land of Egypt; open your mouth wide, and I will fill it. But My people would not heed My voice, and Israel would have none of me. So I gave them over to their own stubborn heart, to walk in their own counsels" (Psalm 81:10-12).

Jude uses a rather unusual word picture to describe those who use others for their personal advantage. They speak "great swelling words" to gain the association. The Greek word is *huperogkos,* which conveys something like "beyond weight" or "too heavy." The words are coming from hearts that are lustful and attempting to manipulate others for their own benefit. It appears that those who "grumble" and "complain" will use "heavy" words to achieve their own ends.

SEPARATE AND SENSUAL

"But you, beloved, remember the words which were spoken before
by the apostles of our Lord Jesus Christ: how they told you
that there would be mockers in the last time who would walk
according to their own ungodly lusts. These are sensual persons,
who cause divisions, not having the Spirit." (Jude 1:17-19)

J ude had previous contact with the apostle Peter and was aware of
Peter's observation "that scoffers will come in the last days, walking according to their own lusts" (2 Peter 3:3). Peter describes the
lusts of these scoffers by pointing out that their derision is focused on
the second coming of our Lord Jesus—they deny the very possibility
of the creation itself and, therefore, the omnipotent and omniscient
authority of God Himself (2 Peter 3:4-6).

Jude, however, focuses on the core character of these mockers,
noting that they separate themselves (cause divisions) and are sensual.
They are "soulish" (the Greek word is the adjective form of the noun
for "soul"). That is, these kinds of people are driven by their "natural
man" and cannot receive "the things of the Spirit of God" (1 Corinthians 2:14). James is even more intense: These people are "earthly,
sensual, demonic" (James 3:15).

Furthermore, they consciously separate themselves from the godly. The apostle John speaks to this phenomenon: "They went out from
us, but they were not of us; for if they had been of us, they would have
continued with us; but they went out that they might be made man-
ifest, that none of them were of us" (1 John 2:19). Jesus simply notes
that "everyone practicing evil hates the light and does not come to the
light, lest his deeds should be exposed" (John 3:20).

It is therefore an absolute: these people do not have the Spirit of
God dwelling in them. "Now if anyone does not have the Spirit of
Christ, he is not His" (Romans 8:9).

∽ 3 ∽

GREAT AND PRECIOUS PROMISES

There is a wonderful promise in Peter's second letter to the people of God. After guaranteeing God's sufficiency to provide everything we need to live in a godly manner throughout our lives, Peter noted that the knowledge that God provides also contains "exceedingly great and precious promises, that through these you may be partakers of the divine nature, having escaped the corruption that is in the world through lust" (2 Peter 1:4).

Please don't miss this. Those "exceedingly great and precious promises" were designed to give us a way to escape the horrible corruption that exists in the world that normally attacks us through our natural desires. What a wonderful gift! That new thing that God gives us is "created according to God, in true righteousness and holiness" (Ephesians 4:24).

Even the Old Testament prophets longed after the coming change in which God would "put My Spirit within you and cause you to walk in My statutes, and you will keep My judgments and do them" (Ezekiel 36:27).

Everything God has caused to be recorded, everything He has done, has been to make possible a life of victory for the twice-born over the awful efforts of the Enemy. Paul told the Corinthian church: "Therefore, having these promises, beloved, let us cleanse ourselves from all filthiness of the flesh and spirit, perfecting holiness in the fear of God" (2 Corinthians 7:1).

Given the following promises, can we do less?

The Colossian Challenge

"To the saints and faithful brethren in Christ who are
in Colosse: Grace to you and peace from God our Father
and the Lord Jesus Christ." (Colossians 1:2)

Paul's letter to the church in Colosse is especially instructive to those who would seek a close relationship with the Lord Jesus.

Chapter 1 provides a breathtaking summary of the purpose for which we are saved and the eternal changes that take place at salvation. "And you, who once were alienated and enemies in your mind by wicked works, yet now He has reconciled in the body of His flesh through death, to present you holy, and blameless, and above reproach in His sight" (Colossians 1:21-22).

Chapter 2 provides clear warnings about the spiritual battle that is taking place and precise insights on gaining victory over the world. "As you therefore have received Christ Jesus the Lord, so walk in Him, rooted and built up in Him and established in the faith, as you have been taught, abounding in it with thanksgiving" (Colossians 2:6-7).

Chapter 3 insists that our responsibility is to take advantage of what has been provided by Christ and to live as *Christ*-ians. "If then you were raised with Christ, seek those things which are above, where Christ is, sitting at the right hand of God. Set your mind on things above, not on things on the earth" (Colossians 3:1-2).

Chapter 4 gives practical instructions for our day-to-day relationships through the lives of the godly people who worked with Paul. "Walk in wisdom toward those who are outside, redeeming the time. Let your speech always be with grace, seasoned with salt, that you may know how you ought to answer each one" (Colossians 4:5-6).

COMPLETE IN HIM

*"And you are complete in Him, who is the head
of all principality and power." (Colossians 2:10)*

The term *pleroo* simply means "to fill up." We are "complete" with the "power that works in us" (Ephesians 3:20). Many passages amplify and reiterate this concept. Once we are "born again" (John 3:7), the creation miracle that is the second birth is sufficient for "all things that pertain to life and godliness" (2 Peter 1:3). As "newborn babes," we must "desire the pure milk of the word, that [we] may grow thereby" (1 Peter 2:2). There is no instant maturity to be had, but the resources are innate to the "new creation; old things have passed away; behold, all things have become new" (2 Corinthians 5:17).

The key to understanding and applying both the authority and the ability of this complete resource is "use." That is, confidence grows as our senses are "exercised to discern both good and evil" (Hebrews 5:14). All too often we apply the declaration "faith comes by hearing, and hearing by the word of God" (Romans 10:17) only to the salvation moment. But that principle is the operative power throughout our lives.

- "The fear of the LORD is the beginning of wisdom; a good understanding have all those who do His commandments" (Psalm 111:10).
- "I understand more than the ancients, because I keep Your precepts" (Psalm 119:100).
- "Your word is a lamp to my feet and a light to my path" (Psalm 119:105).

We are "filled up" because "all the fullness" dwells in Christ (Colossians 1:19). We have been given "exceedingly great and precious promises, that through these [we] may be partakers of the divine nature, having escaped the corruption that is in the world through lust" (2 Peter 1:4).

RISEN WITH CHRIST

"If then you were raised with Christ, seek those things which are above, where Christ is, sitting at the right hand of God." (Colossians 3:1)

The twice-born have been raised with Christ and the "new man" is effectively positioned with Christ in glory. We have been made alive "together with Christ" (Ephesians 2:5) and in the eternal reality of our Creator, who "made us sit together in heavenly places" (Ephesians 2:6).

Thus, the command to seek the "above" realities is not merely a theological idea but rather a profound order to embrace the reality of our new empowerment to walk with Christ in a new life (Romans 6:4). Indeed, we have been newly created by the Creator in "true righteousness and holiness" (Ephesians 4:24). Therefore, since we are God's workmanship, it is not possible that God could create His children for any other purpose than "good works" (Ephesians 2:10).

Obviously, our Lord knows that we are still in "earthen vessels" (2 Corinthians 4:7). That is precisely why He promised to provide all of our earthly needs if we would but "seek first the kingdom of God and His righteousness" (Matthew 6:33)—including our necessary "patient continuance in doing good" (Romans 2:7). Remember, "God shall supply all your need according to His riches in glory by Christ Jesus" (Philippians 4:19).

The environment of the world constantly opposes the reality of "above." Even the wisdom of above seems counterintuitive; it is "first pure, then peaceable, gentle, willing to yield, full of mercy and good fruits, without partiality and without hypocrisy" (James 3:17). Yet, we are still expected to seek to live like we are above, because "the life which I now live in the flesh I live by faith in the Son of God, who loved me and gave Himself for me" (Galatians 2:20).

Focus Your Mind

"Set your mind on things above, not on things on the earth." *(Colossians 3:2)*

The command of this verse is contained in the Greek word *phroneo*. The noun form has an emphasis on the emotive side of our thoughts. Its use in secular Greek literature favors what we might call our gut reactions or intuition. Obviously, the verb is recorded in the imperative mode, making the term both intensive and authoritative. It could well be translated "Direct your reactions so that they respond to" heavenly matters.

The Lord Jesus rebuked Peter because he was not mindful of the things of God (Matthew 16:23). In many places, the translators have chosen "mind" as the term's best rendering (e.g., Philippians 2:2, 5; 3:15-16; 4:2, 10). But in each case, the emphasis appears to be on the way we react to our relationship to God's Word or to each other.

And in each case, as in this text, the emphasis is always for us to focus on the matters of eternity, not on our earthly circumstances. Paul's great teaching throughout Romans 6, 7, and 8 gives a wonderful comparison and contrast between the flesh and the spirit, concluding in chapter 8 that "those who live according to the flesh set their minds on the things of the flesh, but those who live according to the Spirit, the things of the Spirit" (Romans 8:5).

Insisting that the believers in the Philippian church follow his own life's example, Paul agonizes over the many among them who walk so "that they are the enemies of the cross of Christ: whose end is destruction, whose god is their belly, and whose glory is in their shame—who set their mind on earthly things" (Philippians 3:18-19).

A worldly lifestyle is very dangerous for a believer. Please remember the warning that "whoever therefore wants to be a friend of the world makes himself an enemy of God" (James 4:4).

PUT TO DEATH YOUR FLESHLY MEMBERS

"Therefore put to death your members which are
on the earth: fornication, uncleanness, passion, evil desire,
and covetousness, which is idolatry." (Colossians 3:5)

This imperative command is very important for the twice-born. It is nothing less than an active execution of passionate, evil deeds born from the lusts of the flesh. "For if you live according to the flesh you will die; but if by the Spirit you put to death the deeds of the body, you will live" (Romans 8:13). The list that follows is unyielding.

- Fornication (*porneia*) includes all deviant and extramarital sex (Leviticus 18:6-23; Romans 1:26-28).

- Uncleanness (*akatharsia*) references that which is dirty, foul, wanton, or lewd (Ephesians 4:17-19).

- Inordinate affection (*pathos*) is a word used only of homosexuality (Romans 1:26; 1 Thessalonians 4:5).

- Evil desire (*epithumia*) describes evil cravings (1 Peter 4:3; Jude 1:17-19).

- Covetousness (*pleonexia*) is simply greediness that is idolatry (2 Peter 2:12-14; 1 Thessalonians 2:5).

This evil behavior will surely bring the "wrath of God…against all ungodliness and unrighteousness of men, who suppress the truth in unrighteousness" (Romans 1:18). That judgment will be carried out on such people because of an impenitent heart that is "treasuring up" the "righteous judgment of God" (Romans 2:5-6).

The most startling fact of this behavior is that those who willfully participate in it know "the righteous judgment of God" and that "those who practice such things are deserving of death." Not only does this behavior signify a rebellious heart but also an open desire to "approve of those who practice them" (Romans 1:32).

"Let no one deceive you with empty words, for because of these things the wrath of God comes upon the sons of disobedience" (Ephesians 5:6).

CLEAN YOUR MIND

"But now you yourselves are to put off all these: anger, wrath, malice, blasphemy, filthy language out of your mouth. Do not lie to one another, since you have put off the old man with his deeds." (Colossians 3:8-9)

O nce the intense drives of the fleshly appetites have been "executed," we who have been created after God "in true righteousness and holiness" (Ephesians 4:24) must cleanse the passions of the intellect as well.

The action required is that we must "put away from" or "throw away" these ideas that are begun in the mind. These notions are sinful and harmful to everyone.

- Anger (*orge*) is an agitation of the soul that generates an impulse, a desire, that produces a violent emotion.

- Wrath (*thumos*), as the word suggests, is intellectual heat, a boiling up that produces a fierce indignation.

- Malice (*kakia*) is the ill will that creates a desire to injure, even eliminating shame at breaking laws.

- Blasphemy (*blasphemia*), one of the few words directly transliterated from the Greek, means any slander or speech that is injurious to another's good name.

- Filthy communication (*aischrologia*) is any kind of foul speaking or low and obscene speech.

- Lying (*pseudomai*) is any deliberately false information.

We are to put off the old man, that nature and behavior that was bound up in the flesh (Ephesians 4:22), and put on the new man "who is renewed in knowledge according to the image of Him who created him" (Colossians 3:10).

Our salvation brings with it both a new heart and a new mind. With the one, we are able to "put to death" the deeds of the flesh. With the other, we are to put on "the Lord Jesus Christ, and make no provision for the flesh, to fulfill its lusts" (Romans 13:14)

WRAP YOURSELF IN GODLINESS

"Therefore, as the elect of God, holy and beloved, put on tender mercies, kindness, humility, meekness, longsuffering; bearing with one another, and forgiving one another." (Colossians 3:12-13)

The verb choice in this portion of the command is different from those used earlier. Here the word is *enduo*, which describes "sinking down" into a garment. It is most often used of a robe or seamless cloak that covers the whole body (Mark 1:6; Matthew 27:31; John 19:23).

There are several passages that allude to this total change of behavior—like enveloping oneself in a body-covering cloak.

- "But put on the Lord Jesus Christ, and make no provision for the flesh, to fulfill its lusts" (Romans 13:14).

- "For as many of you as were baptized into Christ have put on Christ" (Galatians 3:27).

- "Put on the whole armor of God, that you may be able to stand against the wiles of the devil" (Ephesians 6:11).

Perhaps an even more precise picture is what happens to us when we are brought into the resurrected and eternal condition that is "like" the Lord Jesus (1 John 3:2). Then we will "put on incorruption" and "put on immortality" (1 Corinthians 15:53-54).

The character traits of God cannot coexist with the "members" of our flesh. They must be "put to death." Neither can godliness control our minds when evil thoughts dominate. They must be put off. Yet for us to put on the character of God, we must "glue" together the character traits identified in this text by love and let God's peace rule in our hearts. Even then, the word of Christ must dwell in our lives richly, so much so that whatever we do "in word or deed" is done in the name of the Lord Jesus (Colossians 3:14-17).

REDEEM THE TIME

"Walk in wisdom toward those who are outside, redeeming the time. Let your speech always be with grace, seasoned with salt, that you may know how you ought to answer each one." (Colossians 4:5-6)

Time is the most precious resource available to us. Obviously, it becomes available moment by moment, and there is absolutely no way to recapture what has moved into the past. "So teach us to number our days, that we may gain a heart of wisdom" (Psalm 90:12).

Our lifestyle should be recognizable from the wisdom that comes from the "fear of the LORD" (Psalm 111:10), so much so that our everyday conversation should not be "in words which man's wisdom teaches but which the Holy Spirit teaches, comparing spiritual things with spiritual" (1 Corinthians 2:13).

"Every idle word men may speak" will one day be evaluated "in the day of judgment" (Matthew 12:36). It is clear that "God will bring every work into judgment, including every secret thing, whether good or evil" (Ecclesiastes 12:14).

That is why we are to redeem the time. The Greek term is *exagoradzo*, meaning to buy up or to make the most of time "because the days are evil" (Ephesians 5:16). Our speech must be consciously planned to "answer each one" in such a way that it "always be with grace, seasoned with salt"—two apparently opposite characteristics.

Our words should be "like a honeycomb, sweetness to the soul and health to the bones" (Proverbs 16:24). "But if the salt loses its flavor, how will you season it?" (Mark 9:50). It is the combined power that is important. "Always be ready to give a defense to everyone who asks you a reason for the hope that is in you, with meekness and fear" (1 Peter 3:15).

REJOICE

"Rejoice in the Lord always. Again I will say, rejoice!" (Philippians 4:4)

This encouraging command has been used in many generations of Sunday school teachings and sermons to challenge the saints. The apostle Paul uses nearly half of the 74 appearances of the word in the New Testament in his epistles.

The simple statement in Philippians 4:4 seems to summarize all of the other passages: Rejoice (imperative command) in the Lord (the qualifier, the "way" to rejoice) *always* (in every circumstance and condition). Joy is a godly thing.

Because of our sinful condition, we cannot easily "rejoice in the Lord." We can have fleeting moments of happiness and experiences that fill our hearts with delight and pleasure, but true joy—the ability to rejoice—only comes "in the Lord."

- "Be glad in the LORD and rejoice, you righteous; and shout for joy, all you upright in heart!" (Psalm 32:11).
- "Rejoice in the LORD, O you righteous! For praise from the upright is beautiful" (Psalm 33:1).
- "Let all those who seek You rejoice and be glad in You; let such as love Your salvation say continually, 'The LORD be magnified!'" (Psalm 40:16).
- "My lips shall greatly rejoice when I sing to You, and my soul, which You have redeemed" (Psalm 71:23).
- "Rejoice in the LORD, you righteous, and give thanks at the remembrance of His holy name" (Psalm 97:12).

In the twice-born, joy and rejoicing produce emotion (gladness, cheering, praise, singing, thanks, etc.), but the object of the emotion is always the source of our joy—the Lord Jesus, our Savior, King, and Creator.

MODERATION

"Let your gentleness be known to all men.
The Lord is at hand." (Philippians 4:5)

The King James Version uses the word "moderation" for the word rendered here as "gentleness." There are three important aspects to this instruction. First, we are to be "moderate," the core meaning of which is to be "equitable" (or fair), with further associations of mild and gentle.

The Greek word rarely appears in the New Testament. Twice the qualifications of church leaders include this characteristic (1 Timothy 3:3; Titus 3:2), both times stressing the gentle aspect of the term. Once the term is used in a broad sweep of adjectives outlining the "wisdom that is from above" (James 3:17)—all aspects, incidentally, fleshing out the idea of "fair" or "equitable."

Secondly, we are told to make our moderation "known to all men." That is very demanding, since it is more difficult to apply equity to all people rather than just attempt to be fair and gentle in our dealings. Surely the Holy Spirit is insisting that our inner characteristic be one of moderation so that the resulting actions will flow from our character rather than our circumstances. As noted of the members of the Corinthian church, they were declared to be "an epistle of Christ" (2 Corinthians 3:3). Everybody "reads" us, and what others decide about us must include the reputation of fair and gentle behavior to all.

Finally, the reason this requirement is so significant is because "the Lord is at hand." Although a quick application might lead one to think this means "the Lord is coming back soon," the time element is not at all implied in the sentence. A better translation might be "the Lord is alongside," "He is close," or even "the Lord is with you." It is easy, sometimes, to forget that God indwells us through the Holy Spirit and that our every action and thought are known by our Creator (Psalm 139:3-4).

ANXIOUS FOR NOTHING

"Be anxious for nothing, but in everything by prayer and supplication, with thanksgiving, let your requests be made known to God." (Philippians 4:6)

Many of us know precious people who seem to thrive on making sure the details are right. They keep us careful, ensure our safety, and strengthen our plans. Yet, that same strength can lead to anxiety, troubling the soul and dominating one's life. The above text warns us of this facet.

Our Lord gently admonished in Luke 10:41: "Martha, Martha, you are worried and troubled about many things." Martha, Mary, and their brother Lazarus were longtime associates of the Lord Jesus. He had spent many hours in their home and had come to love them as close friends. No doubt Martha had often prepared for Christ's visits and had been "in turmoil" over the details many times. But our gracious Lord saw the circumstances controlling Martha and softly insisted she not lose the thing of greatest value by sacrificing the permanent on the altar of the immediate.

That is the admonition in our text. Nothing should absorb us so much that we attempt to solve things on our own before submitting our requests to our Lord. Jesus made it pretty clear: "Do not worry about your life, what you will eat or what you will drink; nor about your body, what you will put on" (Matthew 6:25). Look around, our Lord insisted. The birds and the flowers can't be altered by our "thoughts."

After all that Job's friends did to "encourage" him, our great Creator reminded Job of the many wonders he could see if he paid attention. Nothing is beyond the care of our Lord. Sometimes, we need reminding, too.

RIGHT THINKING

"Finally, brethren, whatever things are true,...noble,...just,...pure,... lovely,...of good report; if there is any virtue and if there is anything praiseworthy—meditate on these things." (Philippians 4:8)

Our lives are surrounded with ungodliness and demands that often bleed away our thoughts until we are worn and weakened. Reflect for a few moments on this inventory of empowering thinking.

- Truth—literally, "that which is not hidden," Jesus Himself (John 14:6), the Word of God (John 17:17; Psalm 119:11).

- Honesty—not just accuracy, but "sober" and "venerable," sometimes "magnificent" or "great"; used of church officers (1 Timothy 2:2; 3:8).

- Justice—righteous, just, right, suitable. "The mouth of the righteous brings forth wisdom....The lips of the righteous know what is acceptable" (Proverbs 10:31-32).

- Purity—morally and sexually chaste; closely connected with holiness. The emphasis is on physical and mental purity (1 John 3:2).

- Loveliness—beauty, friendship, delight, and wonder are all suggested by this word (Luke 12:27).

- Good News—this takes discipline because there is far more bad news than good in this world. We are admonished to take "inventory" (dwell on, recall) the good reports (Proverbs 25:25).

These excellent and praiseworthy matters should dominate our thinking in a conscious focus on the attributes in this "final" list. If we do so, God promises His peace in our lives.

RIGHTEOUS BOLDNESS

"The righteous are bold as a lion." (Proverbs 28:1)

A holy boldness is imparted to those who seek to speak the truth of God (Acts 4:31). The miracle of the Pentecost outpouring of the Holy Spirit was followed by several incidents where the various apostles and early Christian leaders spoke "boldly in the Lord" (Acts 14:3, etc.). Where does this boldness come from?

The Presence of the Holy Spirit: The Sanhedrin "saw the boldness of Peter and John" when they were dragged before them (Acts 4:13) after they had healed the lame man shortly after Pentecost. Peter was "filled with the Holy Spirit" (Acts 4:8). He boldly answered the farcical questioning of those self-righteous leaders, and they "realized that they had been with Jesus" (Acts 4:13). When we speak with God's authority, we speak boldly.

The Words of God's Word: The first church prayed "that with all boldness they may speak Your word," and they were enabled to speak "the word of God with boldness" (Acts 4:29, 31). When Paul was starting the church in Ephesus, he "spoke boldly for three months, reasoning and persuading concerning the things of the kingdom of God" (Acts 19:8). We should have boldness when we have the opportunity to "make known the mystery of the gospel" (Ephesians 6:19).

The Assurance of a Righteous Life: "According to my earnest expectation and hope that in nothing I shall be ashamed, but with all boldness, as always, so now also Christ will be magnified in my body, whether by life or by death" (Philippians 1:20). Several godly traits of righteous men are given in Hebrews, "so we may boldly say, 'The LORD is my helper; I will not fear. What can man do to me?'" (Hebrews 13:6).

This is where our boldness comes from.

THE BOOK OF BEGINNINGS
A Practical Guide to Understanding Genesis

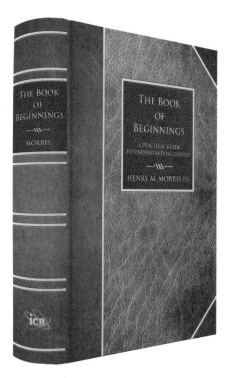

- Expanded Hardcover Edition
- Extensive Subject and Scripture Indexes
- A Beautifully Illustrated Classic Keepsake!

In this comprehensive edition of *The Book of Beginnings,* Dr. Henry M. Morris III addresses the difficult issues in the Genesis record. These in-depth answers will give you confidence in your study of the Scriptures and help you communicate the richness of Genesis to those around you.